WHITE MORNING

JUDITH BERKE

Wesleyan New Poets

WHITE
MORNING

JUDITH BERKE

WESLEYAN UNIVERSITY PRESS
MIDDLETOWN, CONNECTICUT

Some of the poems in this book, sometimes in slightly different forms, originally appeared in *The Antioch Review, The Atlantic, Black Warrior Review, California Quarterly, Carolina Quarterly, The Carrell, The Denver Quarterly, The Georgia Review, The Iowa Review, The Kenyon Review, The Little Magazine, The Missouri Review, New Letters, New Orleans Review, The New Republic, The Ohio Review, Partisan Review, The Poetry Miscellany, Shenandoah,* and *Southern Poetry Review.* "Custody" and "The Retreat" originally appeared in *Poetry.* "The Red Room" appeared in the anthology *The Poet Dreaming in the Artist's House* (Milkweed Editions, 1984).

All inquiries and permissions requests should be addressed to the Publisher, Wesleyan University Press, 110 Mt. Vernon Street, Middletown, Connecticut 06457

Library of Congress Cataloging-in-Publication Data

Berke, Judith.
White morning / Judith Berke.—1st ed.
   p. cm.—(Wesleyan new poets)
   ISBN 0-8195-2173-6 ISBN 0-8195-1175-7 (pbk.)
   I. Title. II. Series.
PS3552.E7215W48 1989   88-38537
811'.54—dc19   CIP

Manufactured in the United States of America

Frontispiece photograph, "Reflection as Completion IV" by Humberto Calzada.

First Edition

Wesleyan New Poets

First printing, 1989

for my mother and father

Contents

I. VILLAGE AT THE FOOT OF THE VOLCANO

We Know Now

We know now the awful snarl
on the face of Gargantua
was a burn, a wound.
The truth was in his slumped shoulders,

the sad inward gaze that is
a gorilla. And yet
we didn't know, knew nothing,

as the moment in '43
when the cruel, inhuman
Japanese soldiers
stepped out of the posters
and bowed so gracefully before us.

How can we go on? How do we stand it?
The dinosaurs lie down
so quietly, so suddenly,
and up come the tiniest lizards.

And we? Later? Do we just
slide quietly under?
Do I choose you? As delicate
as a Himalayan monk?

Who will tell us? The moon,
not even alive, and pulls so terribly on our bodies,

the cells, the genes below that
singing only
blue eyes, blue eyes, blue eyes . . .

Poem Beginning in the Bed of My Mother and Father

If I am the wedge
I am also the pillow
between them, there
in the crack where the beds

come together. Perhaps
even then I think
I can join them
like the piece of flesh

between Siamese twins.
Perhaps when I'm not there
he is holding her
from in back, like the two

waves, the dark and light
of a Chinese symbol.
Or maybe they're
back to back

as helpless as any
instruments
of torture—
but right now the sun

comes in, leafy and sweet
as it is in winter, in the morning.
It is perfectly safe
to look into

the two faces —
and no, I am not them —
the "no" and the "I" tell me,
and yet I am sinking into them

like butter.
Disappearing into
the softness between them.
Maybe that's what we look for

our whole lives: the absolute
separateness,
at the very moment
we disappear into each other.

Completely Open

John dries himself off
after the shower, lies
on the bed, on his back
with his knees up, and I understand
he is the baby now
just for a few minutes, I
am to powder him. Later
I let him cut my hair
a little and then
cut his, just on the sides
where it's ragged.
When my breathing gets tight
he walks on my back,
holding on to the headboard
so as not to be too heavy.
All day in the sunlight
we polish each other,
bare our throats to each other.
Who can understand it?
We sit in the middle
of all this symbology
in a sort of stupid wonder,
as if we had gone into a forest
and eaten all the mushrooms
and none of them had been poison.
We make small barking noises.
Even when we don't touch,
the sounds we make
are not exactly human.

Village at the Foot of the Volcano

The tour guide has brought back the candle
shaped like a woman: *Look, it won't light*
and he holds a match up to the wick
and it fizzles. *Yes, but look*
you still have the woman, says the candle-
maker, and there she is, her wax arms raised
to the sky, smiling.

The candlemaker is also the undertaker. *Yes*, he says,
but when the mountain speaks it also takes care of
the . . . departed. The word he doesn't use
sits there the way a mole sits on the face
of a woman, and she removes it and removes it
and it comes back—so finally she takes an eyebrow
pencil and draws a heart
over it.

We walk back to our tiny hotel
through a series of gardens. The grass here is left
to grow wild, like the hair of the dead.
We've used the word dead here these past few days
more than in maybe a year.
The path in front
of the hotel is cracked as an old face, and dry and

we sit here: each with an empty
wineglass, singing
like the bird who sits
on a thousand-year-old egg
and is happy.

The Retreat

The jobs were quicksand,
he said. The wives were those branches
he could never quite get hold of.
The last time, he darkened the house
and thought of a candle.
For three months he did this. Seeing
no one. Speaking to no one.
On the floor in the tailor position,
his face getting more and more animal
despite him.

I am grateful he let me come.
We sit on the floor on mats
and have tea, a little cold now,
and biscuits that smell of ginger.
He says he is better now. Calmer.
And he does sound it, though I can hear
another voice underneath
like the ghosts you see on TV.

What is that strange tree?
I ask. He says it *looks* like a mangrove
though they were torn out of here long ago
to make a nice quiet street
like this one.

They say the mangrove can live anywhere.
Grows its roots in the air
so it's able to live
where no other tree can.
Like my friend. Like a man I heard of once
who lived his whole life with his heart
outside his body.

Vizcaya

the Deering estate

You almost hate to walk in these gardens,
they're so pure, so French in that way—abstract—
but we do, stopping to take pictures
as though we were tourists at Versailles,
or the Villa d'Este. Facing towards us
is the house, made of the bones, or is it the skin,
of how many Venetian palazzos.
And here is Mr. Deering, so dapper—
1910, he can afford
a little culture now, so he starts importing
gondolas, and peacocks, and statues
of peacocks. Stone faces of huge bearded
explorers, gazing out over Biscayne Bay
thinking, What went wrong?
This isn't the fountain, in fact
I'm tired, and it's hot, and where am I
anyway? . . . They say Mr. Deering liked to dress
as an explorer. Sat in the corners watching,
being shy. The guests
in their splendid Greek and Arabian
costumes. The house dressed
as an Italian, when all along
the bones were made of limestone, and key-
stone right out of south Florida.
Someone stops to take our picture—
my friend's and mine. Trying not to bother
the broad-leaved arrowheads, and the African
violets . . . Under here
are the runaway slaves, and the Indians.
On their sides, listening.
White now. Almost completely white.

Hasidic Wedding

When I speak of the bride and groom
in their wooden chairs, hoisted up
over the heads of the guests, I speak
of crazy joy, though it's true
the women wear wigs, and the men,
too, cover their heads, as if righteousness
lies in what isn't
animal. It's true the men don't dance
with the women, just as it's true
the couple's faces are almost too brilliant
to bear, like white hot wax
from a candle. Still,
if I wanted to tell you the movement
of joy, it would be these
two, their arms held out
to each other—high up
over the wedding
in their chairs; the guests
showing them what it's like.
Pitching and whirling and rocking
them. Dreaming *they* are
the ship. Dreaming this the whole
ocean.

The Invention of the Printing Press

A few facts went out.
Not the truth necessarily:
for that you need a face,
an expression.
Like the time I told a man
a poem wasn't about us,
and it wasn't, in the way one
dead yellow flower
is much like another.

A troubadour
could have told it better:
out in the meadow,
shining over us
like a sun, or a trumpet
and everyone
would be singing.
Though the news
would be mostly about kings.
We, being ordinary,
would only look up, and wonder.

When my old friend died
I could have sung about that
at the campfire,
under my breath, softly.
And people might turn their heads
all at once, as the deer do,
might pick up the tune,
thinking it a song about being alive,
not knowing why
they felt so sad
when they sang it.

Where They Are Now

for Penny, for Peggotty, and for Lois

What I don't understand
is why the room is the same,
in fact the three friends
are up there, each in an old room
dusting, sweeping it clean
with a sleeve. Though Peggotty
is ironing. She liked that. Dozens
of pathways to get one collar
right. Probably it's a house
but I only see these three
rooms, lit up as the brain
lights when you want to move
from one place to another.
Stop thinking of them, someone
on the phone says. Is there a house
higher than this, they could go to,
is it our talking keeps them
ironing like that? When we sleep
I'm afraid the house gets dark
so I stay awake.

Peggotty, her hands on her hips,
laughing. They have to get
all the people from the rooms
to this one table. The sun
is beneath them so their feet
are bare, even when it's cold here,
at night. I think maybe they think
of us kindly, or maybe
not at all; maybe that's what's
hardest: parts of you, rolling
away like mercury,

just when you thought the past
was most solid, and yet
it would grow and change,
the way a rainmaker
sends his voice up to the sky
and it comes back as rain.

Old Woman

A white morning.
A gull lifts, silent,
into the sky. I watch
the old woman,
there in her chair
by the edge of the sea.
She turns, and I see her eyes —
dark, the color
beginning to leave them —
and suddenly I am she —
my hands bony
in my lap.
Talking to this middle-
aged woman, explaining
the misunderstanding
with my body . . .
How this morning
I ran into the sea,
only my body
kept trailing behind,
the way it is in the mountains
when you call out,
and your voice
comes back to you, after . . .
I am telling
the woman, using my hands
to show her these two
things: me
and my body.
My hands
used to be very white,
like yours,

I'm saying, but she
is backing away,
the way a wave does
just when it reaches you . . . I
am backing away
from the old woman,
who keeps talking
about waves, about echoes . . .
or rather we're sitting
side by side,
that is I think
she's still there,
watching the waves in the steady
sunlight.

The Shell

must have come from another ocean.
The Florida shells are teeth
where this was smooth enough that an animal
had been carved there. The real
animal was gone
and here was this profile of a horse
as if someone taking the animal out
had felt bad
and brought it back larger.

We listened for the sea
in it, but the real sea kept drowning it out.
We hadn't seen a shell on this beach for years.
If an Indian had come by
it would have been no less strange—
and we would give him the shell
and he would give us the beach
and we would think
for a while we owned it.

Last Tango

Some children were signaling from the rooftops,
using their arms and legs as language —
it seemed so right and so clear
I thought I would climb up there and call
you, and you would answer.

Ah, the brain is clever and it's lazy.
In the movie the two meet in an empty
apartment. No language, they say,
no past. And the mind takes the grunts
and makes a road of that,

and everything we did or said was a road —
that is the stone sinking. *Love,* we said, *open,*
and the mind goes white, the mind swings open
like a heaven. Listen, outside, a bird
that doesn't belong here. Some

others are driving it out, a counterpoint
lovely only in its sound. Still
I'll listen, I'll have it . . . No power that night.
You ran up fourteen flights, the door opened . . .
Yes, perhaps there desire stopped. Not

when the man's voice cried out, and mine
like a bird's, higher, but somewhere
in between. Silent. So that from there to here
there is no road. No pathway.

for John

Composite (for a second cousin)

You remember Aunt Ray was always
so shy, like a folded-up letter—
and here she is almost gone, one hand out
as if begging for absolution,
a sin so small there's no name for it.
We cousins keep putting our ears to her mouth
trying to catch anything, a whisper,
a brushstroke, I guess, for that composite
portrait we've been trying to keep
of this family; of all of us.
I think Aunt Ray would be the hands:
how she sat at the table,
the tips of her fingers meeting
in a kind of arch
under her chin, a sort of doorway
to catch the words in.
As though our words were important.
How especially quiet
she was then, as if the keeper of words
shouldn't make them. She might have been
one of those Roman women
two thousand years ago
who wove, or sewed, or made clay urns:
the grooves so deep and clear
a scientist could break off a piece
and play it like a record . . .
and there would be that moment:
their looms, the beads they were wearing.
The stories the elders
told of the ancestors.
Everything in that small room echoing
like a canyon.

II. THE RETURN

The Return

When he steps inside it's
the white room, the one
broken blind. The woman
is there with a look of
dust, of aloneness. The dog
approaches, and goes back,
uncertain. The man begins
helping her with the tablecloth:
shake it out, fold it, it's
a little dance, a little
dance, though there are words
he can't remember, like the
taste of something eaten
with little pleasure. The sun
turns around them without
a sound. He keeps looking into
her face to see if there's
a world there he can be sure of.
Get the dishes, she says.
It begins to make sense: he
remembers mornings clawing up
out of sleep as if it were
the ground, the look of
amazement as they found
each other; the room could
have traveled a thousand
miles while they were sleeping,
a thousand miles and he
wouldn't know it, yet here
is that same woman, and again
he imagines that she
is beautiful.

Jonah

For courage,
I tried to eat the heavy flesh
nearest the fish's heart—
but think, after finding a kind
of house in the sea,
of taking the wood from that house.
Think of the poor fish, bellowing,
not in pain, but as if all along
it had *wanted* this invasion,
as your blood might love the part of it
that ate up the poisons.
What could be worse for a man
than embarrassment?
There goes a man, people say:
whatever he says
it will come out different.
That is why I stay
all day at the taverns.
Drink the wine as the fish drank me:
here, on my face, are the blossoms.
And if I told you the sun could stop
right now—there—at the edge of the sky?
That it can scorch a man like a tree?
That if he is wicked enough
the rain will come to heal him? Days now
I've watched the rain, not thinking
these are the tears of heaven,
no, just wanting some kind of cloak
for my head, a coat perhaps of many
colors—yes, let it come down
till there is a flood.
I will make my own ark

this time, and people will say, Take me.
Look, they'll say, he isn't a clever man,
but he always comes back.
By his colors, we know him.

Courtesan

A man wants his woman like woven gold.
Like the lining of his dark kimono.
Like the artist's most elegant
paper . . .
        I sit in the sigh of the old tree.
The girl with her squirrel cheeks
waits at my feet. No one comes.
I who play the instruments like a goddess.
Whose hips murmur like lutes.
Ah, little cricket, you sit
in your web of a box, and I in mine.
If I leave it is naked as you, poor singer,
and my breasts no longer chrysanthemums.
Those years of the magical scrolls!
When I brushed them away like so many
tiers of snow. Even his whose print
is still in my fingers. Sometimes
I look out past this life, these screens,
and imagine a voice that would lift me
out of this flatness . . .
But come, they still speak my name
from garden to garden. Come, Child.
I will teach you to smooth your hair
into wings. To paint your mouth
like a small question.

after a Japanese print

The Wild Child

after the movie by François Truffaut

Finally he sleeps on top
of the bed, though some nights now
he is out under the stars,
swaying from a branch like the tongue
of a great clock.
                    Three months
and he has learned to match a thing
with its symbol drawn on the table:
these scissors, for instance.
Has learned his name: *Victor.*
Listens now, his teeth bared as if he heard
with them.

Today he has done well with the words
and is drinking his milk,
bringing the bowl slowly
up to him. Though it seems sometimes
he would like to spill it,
roll around on the floor, taking it in
that way.

Sometimes the teacher is as kind
as the lady housekeeper. He takes
their hands, places them over his heart,
throat, each cheek, his hair . . .
As if the blood flowed just upward.
As if he had to hold a number
of lives inside him, and he might
die from them, they were that
human.

Ginger and Me

They ask how you learn to walk
in the dark
and I feel their eyes touching me.
I tell them how when you reach
a wall
the air is suddenly thick.
How the cane is my middle finger.
What about color?
What about light?
Don't you carry voices
into the night?

Ginger says she can taste colors.
She can breathe the sky.
I can tell she's smiling
from half a block.
We park at our spot on Third
and sing up a blizzard—
the cup spinning with coins.
We shape faces to go with
the sounds of the feet.

At my place we talk
about the days back in Nebraska.
The sky so big and empty
it could knock you over.
How the crowds here can be
like arms around you. Ginger
says what's the difference,
and it's true, she
would go anywhere—
like a hat.

They ask what it's like
when Ginger's gone,
when the TV's off
and it's night. See—
if you're in a lit-up
house, going down to the basement
you might, near the bottom, hang
on the rail.
I just slide my hand down,
smooth as a coin,
and count steps.
It feels just a shade darker.

The Red Room

What Matisse could have done
with this miserable afternoon!
First of all he would blur the couple's faces.
Then take out other distractions
like flying dishes, howls, screeches, clocks.
Then he would paint almost everything red:
the walls, the cat, the couple's hair—
red as an open mouth.
He would move the man to a lake
where he would drop stones—
his face scattering and coming together in the water.
The woman would sigh,
an aura around her
like the infinite scrollwork of trees.
Her face white, and still, and without tears.
A small figure: closed as a Japanese fan.

And yet there would be hope.
The tablecloth alive on the table.
Bushes, clouds, the sky
trembling at the window
as if waiting
for the woman to realize her grace
as she bends there.
For the man to come back—
as sweet in her eyes as the lake.
For the child to wake up
from his dreams of blackness and blood and silence.
For the world to come into this red room
without smashing the delicate glasses.
The sun first
carefully through the pane.
Then the man—large and dark in the doorway,

and the cat leaping,
and red suddenly quivering
in the woman's cheeks.
Like that part of the fire that remains longest.

Ms

This desk is an antique: it's dainty,
and has limbs, and boy are they shaky.
My boss is a woman, and luckily,
she got this really nifty desk for her office,
maybe to make up for something.
Today when I brought in coffee,
Mr. Tull was in the small chair, and
Mr. Royce on the desk, and then
Mr. Chagrew on the windowsill, you
know, like steps, so the big
boss just stood there and loomed
over them. I brought the messages in,
all folded up, like she likes them. The one I
wrote said: Maybe we should put a chair up
on the ceiling? That she kept stabbing at
like a shish kebab, maybe to keep
from laughing. Then she said, Violet,
get a more comfortable chair for Mr. Ruby
(he's the president), so I knew then
we had to put them in just
the right order, sort of like checkers
or musical chairs; and that's the way it is
here — everyone moves one over. Once I said
to my boss, Did you ever see the TV show
about the baboons? Actually my boss looks
like Jane Goodall — you know, delicate, except
of course she's part of the tribe now.
That's why she wears the jacket
with the shoulders. Sometimes we eat lunch
here in her office, and there she is,
her head back in the chair, swiveling,
and the jacket, like another person,
in back of her.

Scheherazade

In the little cave the bones glow
as if the skin were still attached to them,
yet each wife, each
skeleton, is arranged
in some ordinary posture:
its arms up, beating a carpet,
on its hands and knees scrubbing
the floor of this place, or here's one,
its mouth open as if wanting to tell
a story. Scheherazade knows she will tell this
story tonight. It was there all along,
like the broken bone the dancer can't feel
as long as she's dancing. At dawn,
when the stories end, everyone is afraid,
even the king. They sit
in the royal chamber, she and the king
at the center, the courtiers on their blazing
cushions around them. She uses her hands
as the deaf people do; the eyes of the others
never leave them. In fact last night
she told the tale of the emperor's clothes—
weaving the threads of air with her hands—
only in this version everyone
is naked. And instead of laughter . . .
tears came to their eyes,
as if some freezing wind
had touched them. And yet the stories
go on when she stops, even the ones
about death. As the voices remain
in the seashells; Narcissus by the pool
with the flower growing out of him.

Rip Van Winkle

The men were puffing so much pipe smoke
into the hall of the courthouse
it looked like the entrance to hell,
it really did. So when they saw me
they just naturally thought I was a ghost.
Listen, I said, *it's me, Rip*,
but it might have been smoke
talking. *Look, I'm real*,
I said, and took out my old knife and cut my hand.
But when the blood started, I could tell
they were disappointed. The way we were
when those creaking noises we heard
weren't the ghost of poor old Hendrick Hudson.
All of a sudden I could see
we needed these tales
as much as the Indians did,
only *we* couldn't come back
like the Indians. Look, that crow
on the little girl's shoulder.
Held my arms out in front
like a sleepwalker
and tried making a sound like the wind.
Later I'd tell them it was only I,
a man. But right now I was a ghost
again. A grandfather. Some old uncle
they lost, that had been lost
to them . . . There was a war
I heard, while I was asleep
but they were so far away, so innocent
up in these mountains,
even the ghosts of the soldiers
couldn't find them.

III. THE CHILD

Learning Greed

The woman who is my mother
comes home from work. I'm three.
She's wearing a fur coat, a hat
with some kind of feathers.
I go to her as a fan would
to ask for an autograph, I rush
to her with all the greed
of the starving, demanding
my gift, her present.
It isn't nice to ask, says
my father, but I want it, I want
it, and here it is—
something fuzzy—a sweater,
angora perhaps, and the powdery
soft cheek, and the soft mist
from the fur coat, and all the vivid
blue air that flashes
around her. That says wait for me,
I'll be there sooner or
later. That says: someone
takes something away, and
they give it back. It may not be
what you want, but you can
touch it, it will be real
like this offering, this pink thing—
so take it.

Climbing Down a Leg of the Eiffel Tower

The wind is trying to blow us away,
my little cousin and me, round and round and
it's half sky, half ground
out there, an angle
only an insect sees, or a goat
maybe and then we're down, and he's gone,
my crazy cousin (some kind of joke
I guess) and I am lost, my first day, first
evening, in Paris.
For the first time in my life I feel
absolutely alone,
as if you looked at a globe
and saw a little figure crawling
forlornly around it. It's
dusk. I can hardly read
the signs, but that only makes it better.
I try to make of each doorway
a sign, each face
in the doorway, as if there's no speech,
only gestures. A policeman
speaks to me with his arm,
the cape like a bat, like a skirt
to hide behind. My mother used
to push me away from her skirts: There's
a nice little girl, why don't you play
with her? This is like the dream
where everything recedes
as you approach it, only it isn't
gray or cold, it's lapis,
the sky, flowing around the circular eyes
of the lampposts. This woman
approaching, waving
a loaf of bread, could be my aunt,
or this next one, tendrilly

like an orchid. What life
couldn't I lead here
though I'm twice the size
of most of these citizens.
What life couldn't you lead
if you let enough go,
if you went by only
the signs?

In the Berkshires

Because I didn't keep my hand flat
the dwarf pony bit into it
when he bit into the apple.
Here's the half-moon
on the Mound of Venus.

Later, as we continued up the trail,
the Dobermans slammed
from the empty farmhouse
like bats from a cave,
only this time I remembered
to hold my hand palm up.
Though I wasn't sure
what that meant, exactly.

On the way back, I was thinking
how there in the mountains
the gestures had to be perfect.

Every animal there is
was out in the sky.
Every hunter and bear,
hunter, and hunted.
All the disharmonies,
but in conjunction.

The sky flowed around us.
No, into us.
Cold.
In our hair.
Our bodies.

The Three Sisters

Nobody seems to remember if great-grandmother had
any sisters. That she came to America is ordinary
as flypaper, but then with a ripping sound
she went back. Imagine: that ship that stank
of loneliness and desire, and now all this
was packed in deeper, a thousand passengers
having leaned vomiting over the side, the way a yanked
rose spits out its seeds from a strange container.
There are the three sisters weeping for Moscow,
but this is worse. For great-grandmother has been
to the holy place—and the dirt
was strange, the words were strange, the small
doorway on Monroe Street; she there, gazing
out steadily, like a sailor.
Great-grandmother, I'm taking you back to the ship
you came on; it never arrived. I'm rowing that huge
ship backwards, rowing that ship
back to Odessa—and as it makes its way back
to the dock there, America is coming back, the dream
of America, only a little bigger, a little
richer. I'm giving you back the dream
as it was—spotless—like the dream
of the three sisters. You can sit in the little
square and talk with the others about
New York, America. The sea birds calling
the news of the ships: those that return; those that go out
again.

The Child

Someone has made a hole
in the floor
and you can see into the room.
The child sits on the bed. You see only
the top of her head,
her arms pale as milk.
You drop through the opening.
She does not hear, folded
into herself, shoulders sobbing.
You call. Bring her a coin
that slips from her hand,
disappears.
Bring her a doll that cries real
tears. She drops it,
the china eyes closing.
You say a name: three notes
over and over,
and she lifts her head,
unfolding, unfolding
on the bed
till she is taller than you.
You tremble. Her eyes blue, half blind,
she lifts you, holding you
carefully as a toy.
Begins to sing in a strange soft voice.
Then louder as she walks with you
through the house
to the faded room,
the old chair,
your head on her enormous, warm shoulder,
the trees singing outside,
she singing your name,
your name.

IV. REPRESSION IN THE AGE OF AQUARIUS

Tapestry

A story
simple as an apple.
The woman, attractive as any sunset.
The daughter, plain as a bush or a pebble.
The husband who is
or isn't the father.
Who has touched the daughter's thigh
and gone mad
as if he was the last log on the fire.
Now you would think
the apartment would be smoking.
The girl in hell. In heaven.
That the two would slip
out of the place
like hairpins through loose hair.
But no. Though the fire crackles
like the devil rubbing his hands,
they all sit quietly after supper.
The girl watching
her reflection in a plate.
The man's face intent
as a burglar, or a saint.
The woman knitting a neck, or a sleeve,
or the entire history of the planet.
Watching the small thinning spot
at her husband's temple.
How it is still the same
after all these years.

Oedipus

After he had unriddled the Sphinx
she was finished, I guess,
though not finally, not the powerful
thighs, the lion-thighs
of the women . . .

So then it was the fathers.
Some cities got built. Some nights now
the submarines move in close, their
huge periscopes — east, west —
and all they find is a lot of people,
sleeping.
        Gods, you
have tricked us, I think. Each of us
half, and too many . . . Though my room
is wonderfully quiet. The cat is
black, Egyptian and clever,

I look out at the stars, yellow
as her eyes, the avenues
of the moon I cannot name, moon that has been
a warrior, a woman — softer
now, looking down at the king

who perhaps looks up for the last time . . .
so that this
shimmering
is what he will always see; then
stumbling across the stones
till his feet are torn, thinking
now he will rest,
will hardly move; he will be happy.
Like an olive tree, or a great tortoise.

Nineteenth Century:
The Cultivation of the Mango

One day the woman had eaten a mango,
having mistaken it for a plum,
having forgotten the taste, which was gray
like the skin of a tree. Years later,
late and hungry, she cut again
into the bitter bloom, and behold
it wasn't green inside anymore
but the color of sun. The taste
of orange, of violet . . .

She didn't know they'd been
crossing the fruit. With their science
making it sweet. She thinks maybe
the philosophers were right:
a thing is only as you perceive it.
How lovely, to lie under the
rushing out of the leaves
of the mangos, to nibble the grass
even if it's bitter, and look up at the stars
even if there are none . . .

Repression in the Age of Aquarius

My friend says, when his pretty student visits,
paintings fly off the walls,
and once one of the little big-bellied goddesses,
the way a button would pop
from a too-tight vest.
Brilliant, he said, when she entered
his night class. I don't tell him
the brilliance seems to be mostly
in her hips—how they beat out the time
like a pendulum, as if to say Listen,
nobody's got forever! No.
I go on about Freud. The noises
in his walls. How he had to track them down
as if they were the repressed thoughts
of a patient. How Jung
preferred to think they were simpler than that.
Further off, yet in a funny way,
    closer.
My friend and his little sweetheart
have hardly touched, ever.
You'd almost think one of them
would go deaf, or begin to stutter—
but no, it's the poor walls
going crazy . . . Now a spear
comes down, and the African mask
next to it. I like to attach to all this
notions of love. That if they kissed,
just gently, the room would be all right again.
I don't know anymore what love is
but I would like *this* to be about love.
Not just the wild part, the eros,
not only the spear and the mask
as if that were all that mattered.

Children

They are there. I can feel them
in my curled hands. Or jabbing
at my ribs. When I water
the plants. When I stroke the cat.
When my neighbor brings a cake.
Even though they taste it.
Even though they cry for more.
I shut my eyes
but my neighbor can hear the voices.
And later. The accusations.
I try to tell them. *I carry you*
everywhere. The air I breathe
is your air. You are here.
I pray for them to sleep.
The gentle breath. The sweet faces.
But they don't sleep.
What they want is me. My
arms around them. My singing
in their ears. Me saying,
I want you. I want you.

Custody

Not because of his line of work,
but because his face is
a tablet on which not much yet
has been written, the judge
takes a dislike to the husband.
The wife is nervous as a bird—
a small bright beak of a woman.
She didn't feed us; and she hit us,
too—the two children are speaking
together, as if there were one
mouth between them. We all wait
for the woman to answer. What
is wrong with her? She is
like a hummingbird stopped
in midair, and there's no flower . . .
At last she says to the girl:
If you want to come home, come
now . . . The room is quiet.
There really isn't an evil
face here. *Please tell the truth,*
she says to the girl. The word
truth gets larger and larger
till finally it becomes as wildly
lit up as a chandelier;
almost a distraction.

Visiting Borges

The whole time the young man reads to him
he is thinking Borges is like his house—
sad, empty—oh not the attic
of course, but the parlor.

The floor has large black and white tiles—
the kind you'd imagine even a blind man
could see, so maybe Borges is lost
in the pattern. The young man is a stranger,
he might be thinking. Big. Probably handsome.
Why should he sit and read to an old man?

He has wondered which house
he will die in—in Austin, Nara, Buenos Aires—
oh so many—as if he had not long ago shrunk
the world
till it fit like a small chamber around him.

Or maybe the young man is right: the old man is
the house, which is also the world . . .
But then where is . . . the world?
Have we lost it?
Are we to depend simply
on our senses?

Surely that is coffee we smell
as we walk
in our bare feet up the gravel driveway?
Surely they are in the same house,
the young man, and the poet . . . ?

Recovery

A woman with a house on her back
down on her hands and knees
as if she was looking for a crack
or a penny.
As if the house was not a boulder
and the door could still open.
A map on the floor
of Spain, and one of Ohio
and she will lie on her back
and paddle
as if the rapids were coming.
The nurse sighs
and says, Put down that razor.
You have cut yourself enough
into the walls,
and the plants die of exhaustion.
The children sing on their rafts,
everyone to sea on the Grande Jatte,
and a bird smashes into the picture.
Dumb bird
thinks it knows where it's going.
Stupidity of feathers
not to plummet into this morning.
The bed rising and falling
like her breath on that first weekend
with the red roof
and the stars
and her arms free to rest at her hips
and her life like a lovely clean sheet
and the room
riding high like an ocean.

Dionysus

We didn't have enough money for wine
so we bought some bottles of Coke
and went to the park, and drank them.
We smashed the bottles on the backs
of the benches. The moon was out
and the fragments of glass shone
like so many broken stars.

I started to dance, with my arms up.
The other men put their hands
on each other's shoulders
and began to dance too, in the Greek
fashion. It was good
we didn't get drunk for once,
but we weren't dancing for that
reason. The trees were wine
and the sky was wine, and everything
that wasn't the wine, was wine.

Soon

for Ricardo Pau-Llosa

I can see it, Ricardo, that city!
Each street wavering, circular.
As streams go. As the still mind
    travels.
The crushers and crumblers gone.
The hiccuping, gulping machinery gone.
Here and there a statue that says
    Walk Now.
We walk in our silent shoes
to the houses of friends.
Where the grass stays rich and thick
without tending,
as once we imagined
the mind did, the passions.
We'll recline on couches: Roman,
I suggest, and the bowls of figs,

and the birds will come—cockatoos, ravens—
and they will remember the tongues,
and we will listen,
as once we gleaned the wheat.
As if each story was ours,
and yet particular.
We'll be faithful as the giant
    fish.
As the wolves. And like wolves
we will lie down
before each other. The game is over,
we'll say. Let us continue.
And up to the stars, flying,
Ricardo. If in that moment
we need to, or want to.

ABOUT THE AUTHOR

Judith Berke has explored several other art forms in addition to poetry. After attending Smith College, she studied painting at l'Academie de la Grande Chaumiere in Paris. One of her sculptures, "Dachau '44," is the only work by an American in the permanent collection of the Yad Vashem Museum in Jerusalem. She studied acting with Lee Strasberg and Tamara Daykarhanova; designed puppets and was a puppeteer; and sang with the Opera Guild of Greater Miami. She won a fellowship from the Florida Arts Council in 1988. She lives in Miami Beach.

ABOUT THE BOOK

White Morning was composed in Bembo, a typeface adapted from the Monotype version of an Aldine Roman cut before 1500 by Francesco Griffo, who later designed the first italic type. It is named for Griffo's contemporary, the humanist scholar Pietro Bembo. The book was composed by Lithocraft Company of Grundy Center, Iowa. It was designed and produced by Kachergis Book Design, Pittsboro, North Carolina.